*Imagine putting
a roaring fire, nu̶
your dog at your ̶
same lovely cosy f̶*

̶ ̶ ̶ ̶ ̶ ̶ Horse Society

*Humour, wisdom and terrier-love wrapped up in a smiling
bundle, bringing you light into any moment.*

Pam Billinge, author and therapist

Delicious titbits for the hungry soul.

Tina Sederholm, author and performer

*A warm hug of a book. A celebration of life's little comforts.
It'll make you want to saddle up, walk the dog, go for a run
and eat buttery toast.*

Laura Gabrielle Feasey, journalist

Best wishes

Kathy

Also by Kathryn E. White

Life Matters: an inspirational and heartwarming
memoir of rebuilding life after loss

Cappuccino, Cake and Chat

Uplifting, witty, ditties and inspirational quotes about
life, simple pleasures and animal comforts

Kathryn E. White

Mole
Press

Published by Mole Publishing, UK – in collaboration with
Claire Wingfield Literary Consultancy

Illustrations by Helen Dowley

www.kathrynewhite.com

To my gorgeous animals, past and present, for filling my heart with pure joy.

Dear friends,

This book wasn't planned. By that I mean I didn't ever expect to write poems, they just sort of happened. Words and phrases come to me at the oddest times – occasionally in the early hours of the morning; often when I'm walking my dog or out running. What started off as silly little limericks for friends, has grown into this compilation of simple verses about the wonderful everyday pleasures and ponderings about life.

Don't worry, though – this isn't your typical poetry book. I've included inspirational quotes – including some from my first book, *Life Matters* – as well as my own thoughts on life to help you along your way. And, the wonderfully talented artist, Helen Dowley, has provided gorgeous illustrations throughout.

I wanted to create a light-hearted and reflective pocket guide to life that you can dip in and out of whenever you feel the need for a virtual hug or comforting words or just to smile. The greatest feedback I had when initially sharing these poems among friends, was from one of my running buddies. "Lovely poem – I've never read a whole one before!" And that was my aim: to share these life observations – that just happen to rhyme – to provide a light-hearted break whenever you need one.

So, pull on your slippers, pour that cuppa and allow the book to fall open at whichever page wants to share its contents and wisdom with you – feel inspired or comforted by the words and pictures you see.

Kathryn x

Life is not measured by the number of breaths you take, but by the number of moments that take your breath away." **Maya Angelou**

When we let go of trying to control outcomes, we learn to live in the flow. Reducing our resistance allows the Universe to weave her magic and create the perfect plan for us.

> *When you open your heart and mind to opportunities and are clear about what you want, the Universe delivers, albeit in its own timeframe."* **Kathryn E. White**

Breathe

Breathe, trust, let go;
feel the Universe's energy flow.
Now the magic will begin,
once you quieten the noise within.

Being around horses, or walking my dog out in the fresh air, helps me to let go and relax. When life gets tough, I go outside, whatever the weather, and reset.

> *I think my love of horses partly stems from the spiritual connection these beautiful animals seem to have – a deep wisdom and sixth sense – which fascinates me...*
> *Being around horses was, and remains, my refuge, my escape. They resonate with my soul, the very core of my being."* **Kathryn E. White**

Horse gazing

I stand and gaze, my heart still pounding from
pedalling up the hill.
He lifts his head, alert, his eyes drinking me in.
Unsure, he seeks the comfort of his grazing
companion.
But, on hearing my voice, he turns;
head lowered, his ears are focused on me.

I close my eyes and inhale long and slow,
imagining golden glittering light flowing through
my crown.
Permeating every living cell of my body, the
energy fizzes and flows.

I direct my thoughts to him and exhale.
He tosses his head, he knows, he feels it too.
We keep our distance, but the connection is there;
the binding force I felt from day one.
Always knowing, always listening;
stay safe my beautiful boy.

Saddling up and riding my horse, whether it's out in the countryside or in the enclosed space of the sand arena, I have no choice but to concentrate and be in the moment.

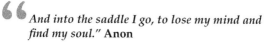

And into the saddle I go, to lose my mind and find my soul." **Anon**

Yard life

Sunrise heralds the start of the day.
The wheelbarrow squeaks as I distribute hay.
Eager faces appear over the doors.
A whinny, a snort – "hurry up!" they implore.

The scent of horse and the feel of leather,
ignite my spirit whatever the weather.
The drum of hooves as we canter along,
makes my heart beat to this, my soul song.

The light fades as the sun drops,
but life at the yard never stops.
Stables mucked out, the horses are fed.
Each contented on their deep straw bed.

A velvety muzzle searches for treats
from my outstretched hand, my day is complete.
Horses are intuitive, they are the real deal.
Powerful beings with a gift to heal.

My first love is eventing, and I'm very fortunate that my current horse, Baz, shares my passion. Eventing is the equine equivalent of a triathlon: comprising a dressage test, a course of showjumps and then the exhilarating crosscountry gallop over solid fences.

> ❝ *The partnership you build with your horses as you train and compete in this sport is incredible. They have to place their trust in you to steer them over the jumps, while you have to put your trust in their athletic ability as mistakes can be very costly to horse and rider."* **Kathryn E. White**

Eventing exhilaration

That one-day-event was an absolute blast,
even though we may have come last.
A super test left the judges a-weeping.
Then into the jumping, and a pole goes a-leaping.
Into the 10-second box we're sent.
"3, 2, 1 – good luck!" And off we went.
Across the country, my fabulous steed flies.
Oh, my goodness Baz, you really do try.
We clear 16 fences then cross the line.
The exhilaration; the gratitude – I'm so glad you're mine.

I truly believe animals find us and not the other way round. My little companion and 'terrier muddle', Mole, is my best friend – and quite the comedian. If I had a pound for every time someone says he looks like Hairy Maclary – the little canine character from Lynley Dodd's children's books – I'd be very well off.

I am so small," said the mole. "Yes," said the boy. "But you make a huge difference." **Charlie Mackesy**

Tribute to Hairy Maclary

There was a little dog called Mole,
his coat all black and hairy.
He had the sweetest kindest soul,
and looked like Hairy Maclary!

Taking Mole for a walk is my daily sanity check. Have you noticed that dogs are always completely in the moment?

Mole strolls

I love my daily strolls,
with my faithful hound, the Mole.
As I take in the glorious views,
any stress I had, I lose.
But wherever we may roam,
there is no place quite like home.

Mole finds tennis balls in the most random of places. I've come to the conclusion, given the timing of their appearances, that they are signs from the Universe because they always seem to materialise when life is feeling a little challenging.

Balls!

I have a little dog called Mole,
who loves going out on his daily stroll.
Off he trots in the warming sun,
for a sniff, and a play, and a little run.
Then on the breeze wafts an interesting smell;
one he loves and knows so well.
Whoosh! He runs into the grass so tall;
to find yet another bloody tennis ball!

It isn't only balls that Mole likes to chase – exercising squirrels is a particular passion of his.

Squirrel exercise by Mole

I am a squirrel hunter,
I chase them up the trees.
But I'm hampered by my trousers;
they're hairy and attract the leaves!

Sadly, Mole has a penchant for rolling in smelly fox poo, too.

Fox poo

Here's a hairy hound-rel,
a dirty little scoundrel,
who loves to roll in fox poo,
goose muck and worms too.
He's really rather stinky,
despite being only dinky.
But I love my hairy hound-rel,
my stinky dinky scoundrel.

Furry purry angel

Harry is a cheeky cat,
always purring and full of chat.
And though it's not nice,
when he brings me live mice.
I'm thankful he's never caught a rat!

Animal comforts

When times get tough and the black dog descends;
when sleep is a struggle, or the darkness never ends.
It's my animals I turn to for comfort and hope;
for a cuddle on the sofa always helps me to cope.

A reassuring purr.
The feel of soft fur.
A brisk walk outside.
Or an exhilarating ride.

There's nothing quite like the love of our pets,
to calm us down and banish our frets.

How many times do our worries grow in the darkness of night? Then when we wake, when the sun bathes the world in light, we realise our niggles and concerns may not be as bad as we feared in the obscurity of nightfall.

Night-time worries

At night we tend to whittle.
It's usually about something quite little.
But in the wee small hours,
This 'thing' develops powers,
and we fall under its spell like a skittle.

Then the dawn brings shards of light,
that shatter the illusions of night.
And we see what we've been fearing,
that seemed so scary and leering,
no longer has substance or bite.

When you feel as if you're battling against life's challenges, taking a step back and being kind to ourselves is difficult. Be assured that you are always where you need to be at that moment in time and light always follows darkness.

When the chips are down

When the chips are down,
it's hard not to frown.
But take a breath, stand and pause.
Look within for a possible cause.
For challenges are how the Universe will teach
us for our highest potential to reach.
Patience – it may take a little while
for us to re-find our inner smile.

Following your heart, rather than the path you feel you should take – or which others want you to – is the first step in ensuring you live your best life and your truth. Get out of your own way and let life unfold.

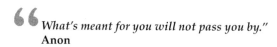

What's meant for you will not pass you by."
Anon

Be free

I want to be free,
allowed to be me.
Be brave,
take that step.
And be free – be me.

Dream and the way will be clear.
Pray and the angels will hear.
Leap and the net will appear."
Christine Kane

> *Contentment comes from our relationship to what is going on around us, rather than our reaction to it. It is the peaceful realization that we are whole and complete just as we are, despite the anger, sadness, joy, frustration, and excitement that may come in and out from time to time."*

Daniel Cordaro

Contentment

Happiness is overrated.
A temporary fix of being elated.
Contentment is the real deal.
Longer term, it's the way to feel.
It's feeling good about what you've got.
Which may – or may not – be a lot.

> *Dance like nobody's watching; love like you've never been hurt. Sing like nobody's listening; live like it's heaven on earth."* **Mark Twain**

Sometimes, those wicked chemicals known as hormones, call the shots, as every middle-aged woman will know. It's like you're suddenly possessed by an emotional, angry teenager. Ladies, this is our very own 'mid-life rebellion'.

> *The menopause is a weird one, as a woman you know that the likelihood of it happening to you is pretty inevitable, but no-one really tells you what to expect."* **Jenny Eclair**

Women-o-pause

Why MENopause when men don't suffer from it? Though I'm sure many would say they suffer indirectly.
I hereby rename it: WOMEN-sweat-bucket-loads-swear-lots-hair-loss-weight-gain-mood-up-mood-down-more-times-than-(w)hor.... mones-heart-races-hairy faces-anxiety-pacing-memory-gone-why-the-****-did-I-come-indoors-o-pause.

" *Yesterday I was clever, so I wanted to change the world. Today I am wise, so I am changing myself.*" **Rumi**

I don't know if it's an age thing, but some aspects of modern life baffle me!

Modern life strife

Some aspects of modern life,
are causing me concern and strife.
Ensuite bathrooms are all the rage.
I don't subscribe – not on that page.
For why would you want to overhear,
every midnight poop and fart and pee,
from whomever it is that shares your bed?
I'd rather they stumbled down the hall instead!

Don't get me started on open plan.
"Knock down that wall would you, Stan?"
Haven't us women fought to be free,
away from the kitchen and domesticity?
Away from the room where we cook and clean,
to relax, to read, in a place more serene.

So shut that door and let me retreat,
to the cosy snug where I can put up my feet.

Peace

Quiet

calm

You know those places you visit where you instantly feel at ease? Walking in the countryside is when I feel my breath deepen and my worries flee.

Water spirits

Hear the water roar.
Feel my spirits soar.
The rushing water is like my mind;
spiralling, swirling, eddies and currents,
dashing, splashing, eager to find its way.

Where?

I walk further along the path.
The rhythmical sound of my feet squelching,
through puddles and mud
Soothing, calming, my mind is easing.
Like the smoke unfurling from the chimneys,
my thoughts evaporate into the ether.

Quietness, peace, relaxation, calm.
On the water's surface, the sunlight glistens.
Finally, to my heart, the soul listens.

Canal capers

I love walking by the canal;
especially when accompanied by my canine best
pal.
A haven for wildlife, you may be in luck,
And see a grey heron or a humble brown duck.

The depths of the lock cause my breath to catch.
My body is poised, I'm ready to snatch
Mole if he wanders too close to the brim.
I really don't fancy that kind of a swim!

Further we wander along the tow path.
The aroma of coffee wafts in from the cafe.
I breathe in deeply, my lungs fill with air.
Taking a minute to indulge in self-care.

These moments are precious and help us to hope,
that when life sends us curve balls, we are able
to cope.

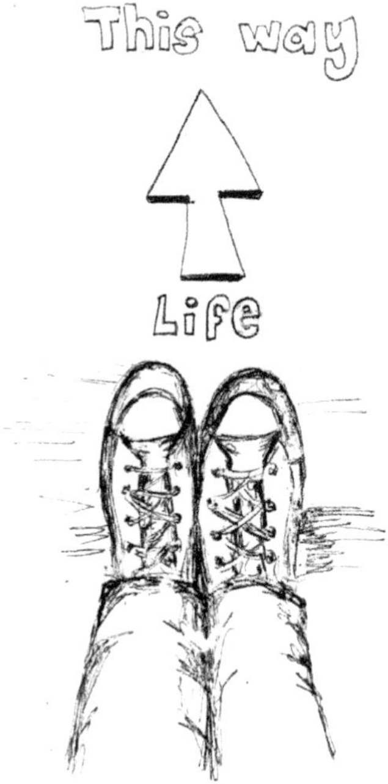
This way
Life

Nature stirs the soul

Nature stirs the soul on wet blustery days like
these.
Standing amidst the hypnotic dancing leaves,
listening to the relentless pitter patter of rain on
your hood.
Turning for home, gratitude seeps through to
your heart,
for the warmth and comfort that awaits,
where the heady aroma of coffee percolates the
air,
And hot buttery toast calls to be devoured.

Another much-loved place of mine for inspiration is
the north Norfolk coast where words always flow like
the tides of the sea. Whenever I go there, I recall the
exhilaration of galloping my mare, Willow, along the
sandy shore for the first time.

Norfolk inspiration

Norfolk was my destination;
to write my book was the motivation.
But as I sat on the sand,
with a pen in my hand,
I fell into deep contemplation.

So, I went for a walk with the Mole,
on the beach, where he dug a big hole.
As I stared into the depths,
I laughed and I wept,
As my story began to unfold.

I scribble and I write,
all day – and all night.
My aim is to get to the end,
but try as I might,
with a deadline so tight,
I'm distracted by coffee with a friend.

Then as the cockerel begins a-crowing,
My creative juices they are a-flowing.
So, I reach for my pencil and pad
And with a flourish, I start writing like mad.
At last, the chapters, they are a-growing.

Simple pleasures

Simple pleasures are all we need.
Immerse in nature to nurture that seed.
Who needs diamonds and precious metals?
When flowers present their beautiful petals.

The tickly sensation of grass between toes.
A moment of quiet; our inner peace grows.
Watching clouds dancing in the breeze.
Or joyful sunbeams shining through leaves.

Stop dashing through life; snap out of that daze.
Just take a few minutes to stop and gaze.
At the world around you – use all your senses.
To absorb the view and drop your defences.

" *The first step to living the life you want is leaving the life you don't want. Taking that first step forward is always the hardest. But then each step forward gets easier and easier. And each step forward gets you closer and closer. Until eventually, what had once been invisible, starts to be visible. And what had once felt impossible, starts to feel possible.*" **Karen Salmansohn**

What are your passions in life? What makes you smile and brings you joy? When I hear country music, my feet begin to tap, and my worries slide away as I become lost in the lyrics and harmonies.

Country to country

Made it to the station,
waiting for the train.
Nothing to dampen spirits,
not even the pouring rain.

I'm going into London,
For country music galore.
Stetson and boots are ready.
Yeeha and heehaw!

I spend most days at my computer creating documents for clients and completing 'life admin'. My perfect escape from the office is having coffee with my friends. A coffee shop is the best 'full stop' at the end of a dog walk; and even training sessions at my running club are punctuated by coffee breaks.

66 *Along with cake," said the mole, "friendship is one of the sweetest things."* **Charlie Mackesy**

Cappuccino, cake and chat

The smell of coffee percolates the air.
We find a table and pull up a chair.
Cappuccino, latte, and peppermint tea.
Sweet treats, savouries – all calorie-free!
Frothy coffee, cake – indulgent bliss.
Catching up with friends – does life get better than this?

I've relatively recently succumbed to the freedom of trail running and this is often when poems form in my head. Maybe the words arise from the rhythmical beat of my feet on the ground and a quiet mind? Whenever you're facing a challenging decision or need inspiration – don't overthink things. Push your ruminations to the back of your mind and your 'Eureka' moment will happen when you least expect it – when you're thinking about anything else but that issue.

Runners' curse

The runners' curse is a curious affliction,
that drives us to run – it's pure addiction.
To move our bodies and shuffle our feet.
No matter the weather; come rain, hail or sleet.

The rain is icy, it stings my face.
I fill my lungs and up the pace.
My nose is bright red, my fingers are numb.
I'm so cold now, I can't feel my bum.

But I'm feeling great, I'm absorbing the vibe.
My heart is pounding, I'm feeling alive!
Splashing through puddles, squelching in mud.
I dream of coffee or a sticky steamed pud.

The rain is freezing, it's turning to snow.
I look at my watch, just one mile to go.
My legs are burning, I'm starting to tire.
As I turn for home and the warmth of a fire.

Make sure, as often as possible, you are doing something you'd be happy to die doing."
Matt Haig

That special time of the day when nature begins to settle for the evening, winding down ready to rest and recuperate.

Dusk

I love this place at night,
when the day trippers have left,
and nature starts to settle.
I love my evening stroll,
with my hound, dear little Mole.
Listening to the birdsong,
and watching the swifts take flight.

And as nature settles for the evening, so can we. Is there anything better than pulling on our PJs and cosy thick socks, knowing that the next few hours can be ours?

Friday night relaxation

Friday night means relaxa-slacks;
a gin and tonic and nibble-y snacks.
Friday night is time to chill;
looking forwards to a weekend to fill,
With fun and frolics and time with friends.
And a coffee or two? Well, that depends,
on whether the sun is due to shine.
And if it does – that cake is MINE!

Our village shop is a fantastic hub where neighbours and friends congregate to chat over a coffee or buy essentials. These little local stores of loveliness bring a community together and offer a neighbourly hug to many.

Community shop

We need the outdoors to help keep us sane,
even when it's windy or pouring with rain.
So, after your ramble or run or bike ride,
visit our beautiful shop – come inside.
Local produce, and essentials we sell.
Gifts, cakes and chocolate as well.
And when you've finished shopping and before you go,
have a hot cup of tea or a cappuccino.
Our seating is outside, but don't you fret,
we have large umbrellas to stop you getting wet.

Often, the things we fear aren't as scary when they arrive as we thought they would be. And there are lessons to learn even during the toughest of times. Through choice, I have spent many a Christmas Day on my own, having spent years dashing around, being away from home and at the mercy of someone else's agenda. I love the tranquillity of my day, while the rest of the world rushes around to fulfil the illusion that is society's mandate for perfect family festivities.

> *Until you get comfortable being alone, you'll never know if you're choosing someone out of love or loneliness."* **Mandy Hale**

Christmas alone

For those who are facing Christmas alone,
take solace and comfort from being at home.
You may just find the peace and calm,
gives you time to relax – like a festive balm.

So let's raise a glass to what we hold dear,
during challenging times, disruption or fear.
I wish you health and all that you've yearned,
as we take on board the lessons we've learned.

*" Life isn't about waiting for the storm to pass,
it's about learning to dance in the rain."*
Vivian Greene

Quotes and sources

" Life is not measured by the number of breaths
you take, but by the number of moments that
take your breath away." **Maya Angelou**

" That first year also taught me an important life
lesson that I practise now daily. When you open
your heart and mind to opportunities and are
clear about what you want, the Universe delivers,
albeit in its own timeframe." **'Life Matters' by
Kathryn E. White**

" I think my love of horses partly stems from the
spiritual connection these beautiful animals
seem to have – a deep wisdom and sixth sense –
which fascinates me…
Being around horses was, and remains, my refuge, my
escape. They resonate with my soul, the very core of
my being." **'Life Matters' by Kathryn E. White**

"And into the saddle I go, to lose my mind and find my soul." **Anon**

"The partnership you build with your horses as you train and compete in this sport is incredible. They have to place their trust in you to steer them over the jumps, while you have to put your trust in their athletic ability as mistakes can be very costly to horse and rider." 'Life Matters' by **Kathryn E. White**

"I am so small," said the mole. "Yes," said the boy. "But you make a huge difference." 'The Boy, The Fox, The Mole, And The Horse' by **Charlie Mackesy**

"Throughout my life, my love of animals, and particularly horses, has been my saving grace." 'Life Matters' by **Kathryn E. White**

"What's meant for you will not pass you by." **Anon**

"Dream and the way will be clear.
Pray and the angels will hear.
Leap and the net will appear."
'Right Outta Nowhere' by **Christine Kane**

Contentment comes from our relationship to what is going on around us, rather than our reaction to it. It is the peaceful realization that we are whole and complete just as we are, despite the anger, sadness, joy, frustration, and excitement that may come in and out from time to time." **Daniel Cordaro, the Contentment Foundation**

Dance like nobody's watching; love like you've never been hurt. Sing like nobody's listening; live like it's heaven on earth." **Mark Twain**

The menopause is a weird one, as a woman you know that the likelihood of it happening to you is pretty inevitable, but no-one really tells you what to expect." **'Older and Wider: A Survivor's Guide to the Menopause' by Jenny Eclair**

Yesterday I was clever, so I wanted to change the world. Today I am wise, so I am changing myself." **Rumi**

The first step to living the life you want is leaving the life you don't want. Taking that first step forward is always the hardest. But then each step forward gets easier and easier. And each step forward gets you closer and closer. Until eventually, what had once been invisible, starts to be visible. And what had once felt impossible, starts to feel possible." **'Happy Habits' by Karen Salmansohn**

Along with cake," said the mole, "friendship is one of the sweetest things." 'The Boy, The Fox, The Mole, And The Horse' by Charlie Mackesy

Make sure, as often as possible, you are doing something you'd be happy to die doing." 'The Humans' by Matt Haig

Until you get comfortable being alone, you'll never know if you're choosing someone out of love or loneliness."
Mandy Hale on GoodRead.com

Life isn't about waiting for the storm to pass, it's about learning to dance in the rain."
Vivian Greene

ABOUT THE AUTHOR

Kathryn lives in the beautiful Chiltern Hills with her horse, dog and cat. She runs a successful medical writing business, Cathean Ltd, to support the development, approval and marketing of new medicines for healthcare companies around the world.

When she's not wordsmithing or horse riding, Kathryn loves running, catching up with friends over a coffee (and a slice of cake) or practising yoga and Reiki.

Find out more and keep in touch with Kathryn at kathrynewhite.com.

If you've enjoyed this book, please help to spread the word and consider writing a review on Amazon, Goodreads, Kobo, Waterstones online or any other suitable forum. These are an immense help to authors.

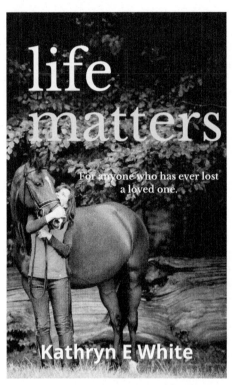

life
matters

For anyone who has ever lost
a loved one.

Kathryn E White

ISBN standard print: 978-1-83804-570-8

ISBN large print: 978-1-83804-572-2

ebook available

Helped me unlock emotions I had bottled up for nearly fifty years. Highly recommended, especially to those who have been bereaved or divorced who will find a kinship with 'Life Matters'.
Vanessa Hill, blogger (Nutty Nags)

Will resonate with anyone who has ever lost a loved one, as well as with people who have a similar passion for horses and especially eventing.
Liz Fussey, Brain Tumour Research

A tribute to the power of love and testament to the strength and fortitude of the human spirit.
Karen Bush, author

Her strength of spirit in the face of enormous challenges shines from every page. As a fellow equestrian, I adored her stories about her horses and dogs. An uplifting and inspiring read.
Amanda Vlietstra, 'Chat It's Fate' magazine

A truly moving and uplifting book.
Alex Wade, author and journalist

Inspirational account of love, loss and healing, illustrating the strength of the human spirit.
Kevin Watson, leadership coach

Written from the heart and soul.
Michelle Higgs, Writers Online

Warm, witty, and honest.
Annick Moon, author

Printed in Great Britain
by Amazon